Happy Holidays

Saint Patrick's Day

by Betsy Rathburn

BELLWETHER MEDIA
MINNEAPOLIS, MN

Blastoff! Beginners are developed by literacy experts and educators to meet the needs of early readers. These engaging informational texts support young children as they begin reading about their world. Through simple language and high frequency words paired with crisp, colorful photos, Blastoff! Beginners launch young readers into the universe of independent reading.

Blastoff! Universe

Reading Level

Grade K

Grades 1-3

Grade 4

Sight Words in This Book 🔍

an	go	it	they
and	have	other	this
big	he	people	to
day	in	so	too
eat	is	some	we

This edition first published in 2023 by Bellwether Media, Inc.

No part of this publication may be reproduced in whole or in part without written permission of the publisher. For information regarding permission, write to Bellwether Media, Inc., Attention: Permissions Department, 6012 Blue Circle Drive, Minnetonka, MN 55343.

Library of Congress Cataloging-in-Publication Data

Names: Rathburn, Betsy, author.
Title: Saint Patrick's Day / by Betsy Rathburn.
Description: Minneapolis, MN : Bellwether Media, Inc., 2023. | Series: Blastoff! Beginners: Happy holidays! | Includes bibliographical references and index. | Audience: Ages 4-7 years | Audience: Grades K-1
Identifiers: LCCN 2022036393 (print) | LCCN 2022036394 (ebook) | ISBN 9798886871043 (Library Binding) | ISBN 9798886871920 (Paperback) | ISBN 9798886872309 (eBook)
Subjects: LCSH: Saint Patrick's Day--Juvenile literature.
Classification: LCC GT4995.P3 R38 2023 (print) | LCC GT4995.P3 (ebook) | DDC 394.262--dc23/eng/20220816
LC record available at https://lccn.loc.gov/2022036393
LC ebook record available at https://lccn.loc.gov/2022036394

Editor: Christina Leaf   Designer: Laura Sowers

Printed in the United States of America, North Mankato, MN.

Table of Contents

It Is Saint Patrick's Day!

We wear green.
It is Saint
Patrick's Day!

A Day for a Saint

Saint Patrick's Day
is March 17.

It is an
Irish holiday.
Others join in, too.

It honors
Saint Patrick.
He is Ireland's
patron saint.

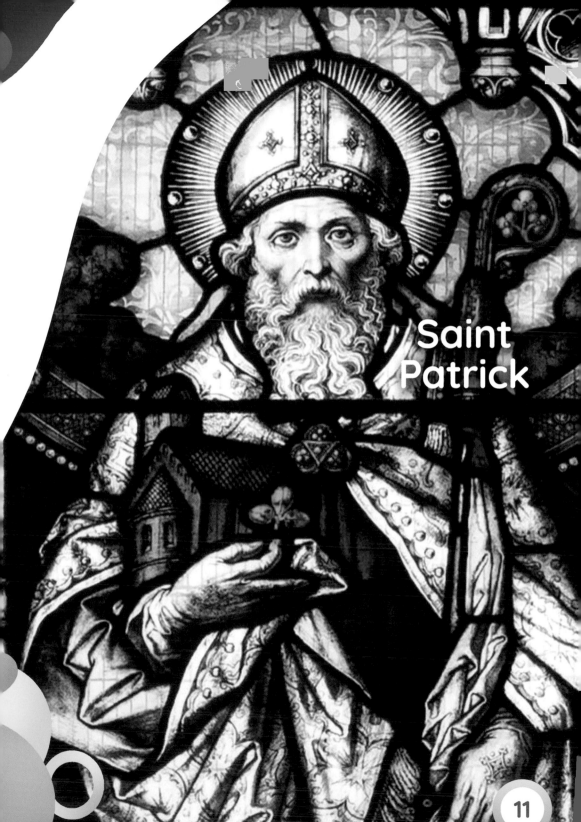

Saint
Patrick

Full of Fun

People wear green.
They wear **shamrocks**.

shamrocks

Some people
go to church.

church

People listen to Irish music. They watch dancers.

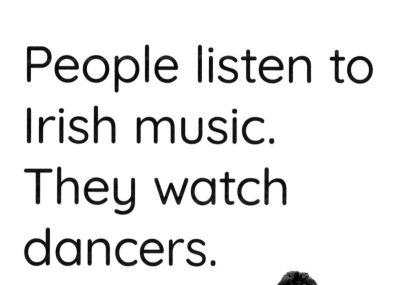

dancer

People have
big meals.
They eat beef stew
and soda bread.

soda bread

beef stew

People watch
parades.
This day is
so much fun!

parade

Saint Patrick's Day Facts

Celebrating Saint Patrick's Day

green clothes

dancers

shamrocks

Saint Patrick's Day Activities

wear
shamrocks

have a big
meal

watch
parades

Glossary

parades

people or groups who walk together during events

patron saint

someone who keeps a person or place safe

shamrocks

clover-like plants with three leaves

To Learn More

ON THE WEB

FACTSURFER

Factsurfer.com gives you a safe, fun way to find more information.

1. Go to www.factsurfer.com.

2. Enter "Saint Patrick's Day" into the search box and click 🔍.

3. Select your book cover to see a list of related content.

Index

The images in this book are reproduced through the courtesy of: AtlasStudio, cover (hat); Olesia Bech, cover (base); Pixel-Shot, p. 3; Natalia Belay, pp. 4-5; Richard Levine/ Alamy, pp. 6-7; railway fx, p. 8; Karlis Dzjamko/ Alamy, pp. 8-9; Andreas F. Borchert/ Wikipedia, pp. 10-11; Raras Yulia, p. 12 (shamrocks); Chris Jackson/ Staff/ Getty Images, pp. 12-13; Charles McQuillan/ Stringer/ Getty Images, pp. 14-15; Stuart Monk, p. 16 (dancer); Phil Crean A/ Alamy, pp. 16-17; nelea33, p. 18 (soda bread); Slawomir Fajer, pp. 18-19, 22 (eat a big meal); Torontonian/ Alamy, pp. 20-21; Sheila Fitzgerald, p. 22 (celebrating); oshcherban, p. 22 (wear shamrocks); a katz, p. 22 (watch parades); Suzanne C. Grim, p. 23 (parades); Nheyob/ Wikipedia, p. 23 (patron saint); Kichigin, p. 23 (shamrocks).